LIFE IN THE SPIRIT

Understanding the Gifts and Operation of the
Holy Spirit

Dr. Charles Dixon

Bogota, New Jersey

LIFE IN THE SPIRIT
Understanding the Gifts and Operation of the Holy Spirit

ISBN 1-889389-09-9

Note: In some Scripture quotations, italics have been added by the author for emphasis only.

Typesetter: Sheila Chang

TABLE OF CONTENTS

DEDICATION

I want to dedicate this book to my dear mother, Mary Tabi (Dixon), who was a single lady while raising me. You have done a great job and your imput has placed an everlasting mark upon my life. Thanks mom!

I also dedicate this book to those in the Body of Christ who have a passionate desire for the things of the Spirit.

PREFACE

Now concerning spiritual gifts, brethren, I would not have you ignorant.
                                                1 Corinthians 12:1

There is no force in all the world whose presence is so to be deplored as fear. Fear is destructive. Fears breeds suspicion, jealousy and hatred. It is fear which sets men (and nations) at variance. It is fear, nothing less, that has kept the world at war, and has hindered progress through the years.

In the spiritual realm, fear is our greatest foe, being Satan's most formidable weapon. Man, unsaved and unregenerated, is kept in bondage through fear of death.

The fear of man bringeth a snare: but whoso putteth his trust in the LORD shall be safe.
                                                Proverbs 29:25

In other words, fears hinders a Christian in his life of service unto his Lord; fear prevents many believers from going on in his Christian experience into the realm of the spirit.

THE BASIS OF ALL FEAR IS INGNORANCE

If the unsaved were not ignorant of the existence and plan of salvation, if they understood the significance and reality of the new birth, their fear of death would vanish. They would then be free to accept Christ and be saved. The same, in principle, applies to the Christian. When you, my Christian friend, receive enlightenment concerning the things of the Spirit, your fear of the supernatural will disappear, and as that fear goes it will be replaced by faith: faith in the things or God, faith in Christ Himself and faith in the things that pertain unto His Gospel.

It is made very clear by our text that we are to have a thorough and concise conception of spiritual gifts also. The gifts of the Spirit are not new. Nevertheless, the gifts of the Spirit in their fullest measure were to be the earmarks of the dispensation of grace, the age in which we live.

It is worth taking note of the fact that when Jesus commenced His ministry, He first read from Isaiah's prophecy.

Now who are we? What are we? Sinners, saved by the grace of God, that's all! Therefore if we are to do the works which He did, we shall have to have, and use, more - much more - than our natural abilities. This thought brings us back to our text, for the gifts of the Spirit are nothing more nor less than supernatural abilities, given of God, to us, that we might be made able to perform the works unto which we are called.

Therefore, if we would be wise, we should study the gifts of the Spirit and all available truth concerning them, their usage, etc., that we be not ignorant concerning them.

The gifts of the Spirit are nine in number; no more, no less. They are listed (by reference only) in the Word.

They are divided by their very nature, and the nature and characteristics of their operations, into three groups, with three gifts in each group. I have listed them in these groups, in their proper sequence, and under their respective headings. These headings are likewise suggested by the very nature and characteristics of the gifts and their operations.

INSPIRATIONAL, WORSHIP, OR UTTERANCE GIFTS:

     1. The gift of Tongues.
     2. The gift of the interpretation of Tongues
     3. The gift of Prophecy.

REVELATION OR INSTRUCTIONAL GIFTS:

    1. The gift of the word of knowledge.
    2. The gift of the word of wisdom.
    3. The gift of the discerning of spirits.

POWER OR IMPARTATION GIFTS:

    1. The gift of faith.
    2. The gift of healing
    3. The gift of the performing of miracles.

INSPIRATIONAL, WORSHIP OR UTTERANCE GIFTS:

    1. The gift of tongues is the God-given ability to speak in languages that you do not understand, and that at your own volition.

    2. The gift of the interpretation of tongues is the God-given ability to bring forth in the language of your understanding, the sum and substance of that which has been spoken in another (to you unknown) tongue.

    3. The gift of prophecy (the product of which constitute the testimony of Jesus) is the God-given ability to bring forth in the language of your understanding - but not via your understanding - a message direct from the heart of God to His people; a message that is always unto edification, exhortation and comfort; a message that always agrees with the Word of God.

    These three gifts are referred to as utterance gifts because of their mode of operation. They are also referred to as worship gifts, because they are principally utilized in the worship of God. They are known as inspirational gifts because their use inspires both the user and them that hear.

REVELATION OR INSTRUCTIONAL GIFTS:

    1. The gift of the word of knowledge is the God-given ability to take unto yourself, at your own volition, a word of knowledge (that is a revelation

of facts concerning things about which it would be humanly impossible for you to know anything at all.)

2. The gift of the word of wisdom is the God-given ability to take unto yourself, at your own volition, a word of wisdom, this being a revelation of what to do about a situation once you know the facts concerning the case.

3. The gift of discerning of spirits is the God-given ability to detect the presence and acertain the identity of spirits to the end that, if evil, they may be cast out.

These three are referred to as revelation gifts because they operate by revelation only. They are also referred to as instructional gifts because of their use the child of God is instructed in his/her spiritual warfare.

POWER OR IMPARTATION GIFTS;

1. The gift of faith is the God-given ability to believe for the fantastically impossible to come to pass at your word, and to pass on, to instill, to inspire that faith in the hearts of others.

2. The gift of healing is the God-given ability to impart the healing virtue of Christ to another (provided they are in a position to receive).

3. The gift of the performing of miracles is the God-given ability to cause to come to pass acts that are contrary to, or beyond the realm of, the laws of nature.

These three are referred to as power gifts because they operate by the effectul working of that power which is in us, the power of God. They are called impartation gifts because by their use you impart something to others. (All these supernatural abilities are operated entirely at your own will.)

Before we go on a step further, we would have you to understand fully the sigificance of the word "gift" as it is utilized with reference to these manifestations of the power and the Spirit of God.

The "gift" is the God-given ability to perform the act, the act differing in each case. For instance, in connection with the gift of tongues, the "gift" is the God-given ability to speak in other tongues at your own will; the act is the speaking in the said tongues. The same principle applies to all the gifts and to your receiving and operating of the same.

With these few thoughts in mind, let us commence our study of the gifts of the Spirit, knowing that we are in the will of God in doing so.

Dr. Charles Dixon
January 1997

PART ONE

THE UTTERANCE GIFTS OF THE SPIRIT

PRELIMINARY

Know that the nine gifts of the Spirit divide automatically into three groups of three; that is, with each of the three groups consisting of three of the spiritual gifts.

It should be further noticed that these divisions are based upon the nature and characteristics of the gifts and the sequence or order of their operations.

The first of these groups, in order of operation, is the group known as the **utterance gifts.** This group is so named because the spiritual gifts which comprise it operate solely by utterance. Let's list them here in their proper order.

UTTERANCE GIFTS

1.   **The Gift of Tongues**

2.   **The Gift of the Interpretation of Tongues**

3.   **The Gift of Prophecy**

Let's study them in that order.

CHAPTER ONE

THE GIFT OF TONGUES

I would that ye all spake with tongues...
I Corinthians 14:5A

WHAT IT IS NOT

The gift of tongues is not linguistic ability.

It is not the comprehension of languages.

It is not the ability to yell, scream or make hideous noises.

The things I have cited above is not the evidence of having received the Baptism of the Holy Spirit. But the latter is the evidence by speaking in other **tongues,** as the Spirit gives you utterance.

And they were all filled with the Holy Ghost, and began to speak with other tongues, as the Spirit gave them utterance.
Acts 2:4

And when Paul had laid his hands upon them, the Holy Ghost came on them; and they spake with tongues, and prophesied.
Acts 19:6

While Peter yet spake these words, the Holy Ghost fell on all them which heard the word.

And they of the circumcision which believed were astonished, as many as came with Peter, because that on the Gentiles also was poured out the gift of the Holy Ghost.

For they heard them speak with tongues, and magnify God. Then answered Peter,

Acts 10:44-46

WHAT IT IS

The gift of **tongues** is the God-given ability to speak in other **tongues** at will. That it is at your will is made evident by the rules and regulations in God's Word regarding its use. Nothing has brought more shame on the Church of Jesus Christ than the much abuse of this gift. Many of the offenses were committed in ignorance. Please remember that our Father would not have us ignorant concerning these gifts.

Now concerning spiritual gifts, brethren, I would not have you ignorant.

I Corinthians 12:1

When we say that you speak in other **tongues,** we mean you speak with other **tongues** (languages) that you do not comprehend. Any language that you do not understand is another **tongue** to you. This is made very plain in the following references wherein the **tongue** spoken is referred to as "unknown."

For he that speaketh in an unknown tongue speaketh not unto men, but unto God: for no man understandeth him; howbeit in the spirit he speaketh mysteries.

I Corinthians 14:2

He that speaketh in an unknown tongue edifieth himself; but he that prophesieth edifieth the church.
                                        I Corinthians 14:4

Wherefore let him that speaketh in an unknown tongue pray that he may interpret.
                                        I Corinthians 14:13

For if I pray in an unknown tongue, my spirit prayeth, but my understanding is unfruitful.
                                        I Corinthians 14:14

Yet in the church I had rather speak five words with my understanding, that by my voice I might teach others also, than ten thousand words in an unknown tongue.
                                        I Corinthians 14:19

If any man speak in an unknown tongue, let it be by two, or at the most by three, and that by course; and let one interpret.
                                        I Corinthians 14:27

This simply means that your understanding does not grasp the significance for the sounds that you utter.

For if I pray in an unknown tongue, my spirit prayeth, but my understanding is unfruitful.
                                        I Corinthians 14:14

For he that speaketh in an unknown tongue speaketh not unto men, but unto God: for no man understandeth him; howbeit in the spirit he speaketh mysteries.

I Corinthians 14:2

I thank my God, I speak with tongues more than ye all:

I Corinthians 14:18

For if I pray in an unknown tongue, my spirit prayeth, but my understanding is unfruitful.

I Corinthians 14:14

This does away with any foolishness such as the so-called gift of languages as taught by some as special preparation for missionary service. Paul was the greatest of missionaries, yet the references make it plain that the **"other tongues"** he spoke were foreign to him and that he did not understand one word of that which he uttered at such times.

By natural linguistic ability, Paul spoke Greek.

And as Paul was to be led into the castle, he said unto the chief captain, May I speak unto thee? Who said, Canst thou speak Greek?

Art not thou that Egyptian, which before these days madest an uproar, and leddest out into the wilderness four thousand men that were murderers?

But Paul said, I am a man which am a Jew of Tarsus, a city in Cilicia, a citizen of no mean city: and, I beseech thee, suffer me to speak unto the people.

Acts 21:37-39

And when he had given him licence, Paul stood on the stairs, and beckoned with the hand unto the people. And when there was made a great silence, he spake unto them in the Hebrew tongue, saying,

Acts 21:40

This latter is not surprising, since Paul was a Hebrew; nevertheless, it was not the common language of the Hebrews of his day, but was reserved for the Temple worship. Hebrew and Greek were not **"other tongues"** to Paul.

CHAPTER ONE
QUESTIONS

1. God has given us the supernatural ability in the gift of tongues for what purposes? List them and qualify with Scriptures.

_____
_____
_____
_____
_____
_____
_____
_____
_____
_____
_____
_____

2. How many attempts may one have in proclaiming a word utilizing the gift of tongues without an interpretation? What should be the course of action of this individual if this should take place?

_____
_____
_____
_____
_____
_____
_____
_____
_____

3. Study Isiah 28:11-12 and explain what the prophet was trying to say about this supernatural ability.

_____
_____
_____
_____
_____
_____
_____
_____
_____
_____

4. What does Paul have to say about speaking and singing in the spirit? Use Scriptures to support answer.

_____
_____
_____
_____
_____
_____
_____
_____

5. How closely does the gift of the interpretation of tongues relate to this gift?

_____
_____
_____
_____

CHAPTER TWO

THE GIFT OF THE INTERPRETATION OF TONGUES

Wherefore let him that speaketh in an unknown tongue pray that he may interpret.

I Corinthians 14:13

WHAT IT IS NOT

It is not the ability to understand that which has been spoken in another language or tongue.

Every Biblical reference to the speaking in tongues makes it plain that the tongue spoken is unknown. If the gift of the interpretation of tongues was the ability to understand what was spoken, then the tongue spoken would not be unknown.

It is not the gift of the "translation" of tongues; there is no such gift. That which is brought forth by its operation is an interpretation: the sum and substance; not a translation, which is a word for word rendition of that which has been given in another tongue.

It is not the gift of the interpretation of dreams. Dreams are interpreted by the operation of the revelation gifts of the Spirit.

It is not the gift of interpretation. There is no such gift. It is the gift of the interpretation of tongues, and of tongues only.

WHAT IT IS

It is the ability given of God to bring forth, in your own language, the gist of what has just come forth in another tongue, whether that message in tongues came via your lips or those of another in the congregation.

11

A proper understanding of this truth will prevent a great deal of confusion.

It is an inspirational gift. That which you bring forth by its use is an inspired utterance. Speaking thus, you do not know what word you will utter next. It is given as you are inspired. This does away with the claims made by some people, such as, "I always have the interpretation, you know, though I don't always give it forth," or "I am sure Mrs. So-and-so did not give the right interpretation.

I had it all the time, though I didn't give it forth." These are ranks falsehoods and can easily be detected as such as we remember that it (the interpretation) is inspired utterance. The interpretation is not received by revelation. You speak as you are moved by the Spirit of God.

In other words, the interpretation is not in existence until it is uttered.

The gift of interpretation of tongues, like the gift of tongues, is entirely supernatural in its operation. That is the person speaking by the operation of the gift of interpretation of tongues is not actually interpreting, but rather is bringing forth — giving birth to — the interpretation.

Literally, to interpret from one tongue to another demands that the person interpreting understands both languages, the one in which the original message has been spoken and the one into which it is to be interpreted.

When a person, by the operation of the gift of the interpretation of tongues, brings forth the interpretation of a message that has been spoken in another tongue, that person is giving forth in the language of his understanding the sum and substance of that which has been spoken in a language he did not understand.

In fact, it is highly probable he did not even know in what language the said message was spoken: this is supernatural indeed.

You who have the gift of tongues are under obligation to pray for the interpretation when you have brought a message in tongues in public.

Wherefore let him that speaketh in an unknown tongue pray that he may interpret.
I Corinthians 14:13

If any man speak in an unknown tongue, let it be by two, or at the most by three, and that by course; and let one interpret.

But if there be no interpreter, let him keep silence in the church; and let him speak to himself, and to God.
I Corinthians 14:27-28

This latter reference teaches us that if, after bringing a message in two or at the most three diverse tongues, there has been no interpretation given, the speaker is to be quiet, he is to keep silence, speaking to himself and to God.

Please note that this is a command of God.

If any man think himself to be a prophet, or spiritual, let him acknowledge that the things that I write unto you are the commandments of the Lord.
I Corinthians 14:37

A message spoken in another tongue with the interpretation equals prophecy in its ministry of edifying the Church.

I would that ye all spake with tongues, but rather that ye prophesied: for greater is he that prophesieth than he that speaketh with tongues, except he interpret, that the church may receive edifying.
I Corinthians 14:5

It is God's purpose in bestowing the gift of the interpretation of tongues upon His people, that by its use messages in tongues might be interpreted, thus making them understandable to the hearers.

The gift of interpretation of tongues is for all who have the gift of tongues.

I would that ye all spake with tongues, but rather that ye prophesied: for greater is he that prophesieth than he that speaketh with tongues, except he interpret, that the church may receive edifying.
I Corinthians 14:5

Wherefore, brethren, covet to prophesy, and forbid not to speak with tongues.
I Corinthians 14:39

But if there be no interpreter, let him keep silence in the church; and let him speak to himself, and to God.
I Corinthians 14:28

Wherefore let him that speaketh in an unknown tongue pray that he may interpret.
I Corinthians 14:13

It is senseless to pray for the interpretation unless you can interpret, that is, unless you have the gift and know-how to use it. God is consistent. He must have intended that all who have received the gift of tongues receive also the gift of the interpretation of tongues; and in effect His Word declares this to be so.

The Word of God is still the will of God. It is evidently His will that all believers should speak with tongues.

I would that ye all spake with tongues, but rather that ye prophesied: for greater is he that prophesieth than he that speaketh with tongues, except he interpret, that the church may receive edifying.

I Corinthians 14:5

It is just as evidently His will that all who do speak with tongues should interpret.

Wherefore let him that speaketh in an unknown tongue pray that he may interpret.

I Corinthians 14:13

Even so ye, forasmuch as ye are zealous of spiritual gifts, seek that ye may excel to the edifying of the church.

I Corinthians 14:12

Wherefore let him that speaketh in an unknown tongue pray that he may interpret.

I Corinthians 14:13

I would that ye all spake with tongues, but rather that ye prophesied: for greater is he that prophesieth than he that speaketh with tongues, except he interpret, that the church may receive edifying.

I Corinthians 14:5

CHAPTER TWO
QUESTIONS

1. Is it safe to assume that all who have the gift of tongues, also have the gift of the interpretation of tongues? Why is this so? How do they work together? Differentiate the two.

_____

_____

_____

_____

_____

_____

_____

_____

_____

_____

_____

_____

_____

_____

_____

_____

_____

_____

_____

_____

_____

_____

CHAPTER THREE

THE GIFT OF PROPHECY

For ye may all prophesy one by one, that all may learn, and all may be comforted.
                                        I Corinthians 14:31

WHAT IT IS NOT

The gift of prophecy is not the ability to preach.

Preaching is the art of public discoursing on the Scriptures.

It is not the art of **soothsaying**, i.e., fortune-telling.

It is not the ability to blast the saints. When a person, purporting to be utilizing the gift of prophecy, abuses the people of God, pronouncing wrath upon them, threatening them, etc., he is not prophesying.

Such a one is merely speaking presumptuously: his personal feelings are being relieved, his utterances are the perilous fruit of the meanings of his own mind directed by his erroneous doctrines.

WHAT IT IS

The gift of prophecy is the God-given ability to give forth in the language of your understanding a message direct from the heart of God to the hearts of His people; a message which is born as it is uttered — not premeditated; a message of edification unto His Church.

But he that prophesieth speaketh unto men to edification, and exhortation, and comfort.
                                        I Corinthians 14:3

17

He that speaketh in an unknown tongue edifieth himself; but he that prophesieth edifieth the church.

I Corinthians 14:4

Remember that in this, as well as in the former utterance gifts, the gift is the God-given ability to perform the act, the act differing in the operation of each gift. This being so, we would ask, "what is the act in the operation of the gift of tongues?"

It is simply speaking language which you do not understand. What is the act in the operation of the gift of the interpretation of tongues? It is the giving forth, in the language you ordinarily speak, the gist of what has gone forth in another tongue, a tongue you did not understand.

What is the act in the operation of the gift of prophecy? It is the giving forth in the language of the speaker, by inspiration, and entirely without premeditation, a message right from the heart of God. This gift operates by inspiration, not revelation. You do not know the message ahead of time. Such claims are falsehoods. Your prophetic utterances are not premeditated neither are they the meanderings of your own mind.

Herein lies the road to fanaticism. The gift of prophecy is an inspirational gift, a worship gift of utterance, not a revelation gift, not an avenue whereby you may claim for yourself or others the things you wish you or they possessed, not an outlet for the secret plans and ambitions of your heart.

True prophecy, the product of the operation of the gift, runs parallel to the Scriptures, sometimes consisting entirely of portions of the same. It is always unto *edification, exhortation and comfort.*

But he that prophesieth speaketh unto men to edification, and exhortation, and comfort.

I Corinthians 14:3

To **EDIFY** is to build up, to strengthen. Anything that tends to edify is unto edification. To **EXHORT** is to incite to a more worthy cause, to lovingly encourage to a more noble endeavor. Anything that tends to produce this effect is unto **EXHORTATION**. To **COMFORT** is to console, to inspirate. It also signifies a state of quiet enjoyment, of consolation. Anything that tends to bring us into such a state is unto comfort.

CHAPTER THREE
QUESTIONS

1. Where can we trace the first account of this gift being used?

_____

_____

_____

2. Who used it?

_____

3. What were the results?

_____

_____

_____

4. What is the Lord's attitude towards we and prophecy? Give Scripture references.

_____

_____

_____

_____

_____

_____

5. Paul often spoke of this gift in reference to the life of Timothy. Find this account and explain how the gift of prophecy influenced young Timothy.

_____

_____

_____
_____
_____
_____

6. How does the gift of prophecy relate to the gift of tongues and the gift of the interpretation of tongues?

_____
_____
_____
_____
_____
_____
_____
_____
_____
_____
_____

7. How is the gift of prophecy being misused in these days?

_____
_____
_____
_____
_____
_____
_____
_____
_____

PART TWO

THE REVELATION GIFTS OF THE SPIRIT

PRELIMINARY

We have just concluded a brief study of the three utterance gifts. These constitute the first of three groups into which the nine gifts of the Spirit automatically divide.

The second group, in order of operation, is of course that of the revelation gifts. These are three in number; I will list them here in their proper order.

REVELATION GIFTS

1. **The gift of the Word of Knowledge**

2. **The gift of the Word of Wisdom**

3. **The gift of the Discerning of Spirits**

These three are referred to as **revelation** gifts, because they function by **revelation.** They are listed in the above order because of their nature and the characteristics of their operations. We will study them in that order.

However, before we commence, let us get the following data straight. No one has ever received or utilized the **revelation** gifts of the Spirit without first being baptized with the Holy Ghost and having received the utterance gifts of the Spirit.

Please do not misunderstand me. I am not saying that you have never received a **revelation** from God. You may have been shown many things by Him. Indeed, you would never have realized your lost estate had He not revealed it to you. For that matter, whatever knowledge of His Word you may have, you received by **revelation** from the Most High.

But we are not studying **revelations.** We are studying the **revelation** gifts of the Spirit; supernatural abilities. If we will bear this in mind, we shall experience little difficulty in deriving from our study that which God desires us to receive.

CHAPTER FOUR

THE GIFT OF THE WORD OF KNOWLEDGE

Apply ... thine ears to the words of knowledge

Proverbs 23:12

WHAT IT IS NOT:

It is not human knowledge sanctified.

It is not an increased capacity to acquire understanding, though one of the ways in which the gifts of the Spirit in operation in us benefit us is in the effect they have in enlightening the mind.

It is not the ability to study the Bible, nor is it the ability to go to Bible school and study the Bible to acquire Bible knowledge.

WHAT IT IS:

The gift of the **word of knowledge** is the God-given ability to take unto yourself, at will, a revelation of facts concerning something about which it would be humanly impossible for you to know anything at all. The revelation thus received constitutes a **word of knowledge**.

We see this gift in operation in the life and ministry of Joseph as he interprets the dreams of Pharaoh's butler and baker in the dungeons of Egypt.

And the chief butler told his dream to Joseph, and said to him, In my dream, behold, a vine was before me;

And in the vine were three branches: and it was as though it budded, and her blossoms shot forth; and the clusters thereof brought forth ripe grapes:

And Pharaoh's cup was in my hand: and I took the grapes, and pressed them into Pharaoh's cup, and I gave the cup into Pharaoh's hand.

And Joseph said unto him, This is the interpretation of it: The three branches are three days:

Yet within three days shall Pharaoh lift up thine head, and restore thee unto thy place: and thou shalt deliver Pharaoh's cup into his hand, after the former manner when thou wast his butler.

Genesis 40:9-13

When the chief baker saw that the interpretation was good, he said unto Joseph, I also was in my dream, and, behold, I had three white baskets on my head:

And in the uppermost basket there was of all manner of bakemeats for Pharaoh; and the birds did eat them out of the basket upon my head.

And Joseph answered and said, This is the interpretation thereof: The three baskets are three days:

Yet within three days shall Pharaoh lift up thy head from off thee, and shall hang thee on a tree; and the birds shall eat thy flesh from off thee.

Genesis 40:16-19

That the interpretations were true the Word of God testifies.

THE GIFT OF THE WORD OF KNOWLEDGE

And it came to pass the third day, which was Pharaoh's birthday, that he made a feast unto all his servants: and he lifted up the head of the chief butler and of the chief baker among his servants.

And he restored the chief butler unto his butlership again; and he gave the cup into Pharaoh's hand:

But he hanged the chief baker: as Joseph had interpreted to them.
Genesis 40:20-22

Since it was humanly impossible for Joseph to have the slightest inkling as to the future of these men, it becomes apparent that he interpreted the dreams by the use of the gift of the **word of knowledge.**

In the course of time, the Pharaoh of Egypt dreamed dreams which troubled him. The Pharaoh's double dream was of fat cattle devouring thin cattle and full ears of corn eating thin, scrawny ears. He could find no one capable of interpreting that which he had dreamed till Joseph was brought before him.

And Joseph said unto Pharaoh, The dream of Pharaoh is one: God hath shewed Pharaoh what he is about to do.

The seven good kine are seven years; and the seven good ears are seven years: the dream is one.

And the seven thin and ill favoured kine that came up after them are seven years; and the seven empty ears blasted with the east wind shall be seven years of famine.

This is the thing which I have spoken unto Pharaoh: What God is about to do he sheweth unto Pharaoh.

Behold, there come seven years of great plenty throughout all the land of Egypt:

And there shall arise after them seven years of famine; and all the plenty shall be forgotten in the land of Egypt; and the famine shall consume the land;

And the plenty shall not be known in the land by reason of that famine following; for it shall be very grievous.

And for that the dream was doubled unto Pharaoh twice; it is because the thing is established by God, and God will shortly bring it to pass.

Genesis 41:25-32

Again the veracity of the interpretation was borne out. The seven years of plenty followed by seven years of famine truly came upon the earth, an established fact of his story.

Perhaps in no other realm has there been as much damage done to the work of God as in the realm of dreams, visions in the night, and faulty interpretations thereof.

It is certain that Joseph could not have known the facts concerning the dreams of Pharaoh, their significance, etc., in no other way than by the use of the gift of the word of knowledge. Only by the operation of this God-given ability could he reach out into the unknown and take unto himself, at his own will, a **revelation** of the facts concerning the problems which confronted him.

CHAPTER FOUR
QUESTIONS

1. In what accounts did Daniel, Samuel, Abijah and Elisha exercise the gift of the word of knowledge? Give Scriptures and descriptions.

_____
_____
_____
_____
_____
_____
_____
_____
_____
_____
_____
_____
_____

2. Which utterance gift works in conjunction to the gift of the word of knowledge?

_____
_____
_____
_____

3. Define this gift thoroughly.

_____
_____
_____
_____

_____

_____

4. Jesus Christ operated this gift often. Tell of some individuals who experienced His use of this gift directly.

_____
_____
_____
_____
_____
_____
_____
_____
_____
_____
_____
_____
_____
_____
_____
_____
_____

5. What gift fits so closely with the gift of the word of knowledge?

_____

6. Which fruit of the Spirit is strongly needed to operate this gift?

_____
_____
_____

CHAPTER FIVE

THE GIFT OF THE WORD OF WISDOM

And Joshua the son of Nun was full of the spirit of wisdom; for Moses had laid his hands upon him: and the children of Israel hearkened unto him, and did as the LORD commanded Moses.
Deuteronomy 34:9

As the gift of tongues is circumscribed in its sphere of operation except the gift of the interpretation of tongues be in operation in conjunction with it, so also the gift of word of knowledge is exercised under handicap without the possession and use of the gift of the word of wisdom.

WHAT IT IS NOT

The gift of the word of wisdom is not human wisdom increased, sanctified, or blessed of God. It has nothing to do with becoming wise, discreet, shrewd in understanding and judgement. The simple-minded can possess and exercise well the gift of the word of wisdom.

WHAT IT IS

The gift of the word of wisdom is the God-given ability to take unto yourself, at will, at your will, a revelation of what to do about a situation once you do know the facts concerning the case. The revelation thus received is known as a word of wisdom.

We see this gift in operation in the life and ministry of Joseph. With reference to his interpretation of the dream of the Pharaoh of Egypt relative to the coming famine (which interpretation was the fruit of his deliberate exercise of the gift of the word of knowledge) we read that he gave the king counsel and advice as to what to do about the situation to the end that life might be reserved.

Now therefore let Pharaoh look out a man discreet and wise, and set him over the land of Egypt.

Let Pharaoh do this, and let him appoint officers over the land, and take up the fifth part of the land of Egypt in the seven plenteous years.

And let them gather all the food of those good years that come, and lay up corn under the hand of Pharaoh, and let them keep food in the cities.

And that food shall be for store to the land against the seven years of famine, which shall be in the land of Egypt; that the land perish not through the famine.

Genesis 41:33-36

Joseph was a foreigner, a stranger in Egypt, sold into slavery by his own brethren when he was but a lad. His education was far from complete. Add to this his years of imprisonment in an Egyptian dungeon without contact with the outside world, and you can readily see that the advice he gave the king was not based on the wisdom of man.

Being a stranger, and uneducated, he would know nothing of the statistics of the country. Its annual grain production and consumption, the amount usually shipped to other lands, would be unknown quantities to him. He would have no knowledge of the birth rate, death rate, record of marriages, immigration, and emigration. In short, in the natural realm he had nothing upon which to base his decision as to what to do about this drastic situation. Yet his advice was so terrific that the Pharaoh, quick to realize the immensity of it, at once appointed him Prime Minister of Egypt.

With the next fourteen years of Egypt's history naked before his eyes (half of that period of time years of superabundance, the other half years of very severe famine) natural reasoning would have suggested dividing the annual harvest into two equal parts, saving half for the years of drought.

By the way, what about shrinkage, and loss by fire and theft? What about preserving a bit of seed for the first planting once the good years commenced again? What about grain required for barter? Oh, there are so many angles to this case; so many things to be taken into consideration. But Joseph declared that one fifth part of the total annual production of Egypt was sufficient to keep each year, in store for those years of famine ahead. One fifth was sufficient, not only for her own needs but for the meeting of the needs of those who might come to her from other lands for help during that time.

Here's another thought. Why did Joseph, a man of God, not urge the king to proclaim a fast? Why did he not suggest repentance and a turning to God as the remedy for the situation? Because the thing was established.

And for that the dream was doubled unto Pharaoh twice; it is because the thing is established by God, and God will shortly bring it to pass.
Genesis 41:32

God's Word decrees

...that in the mouth of two or three witnesses every word may be established.
Matt. 18:16B

It was too late to prevent the proclamation from coming to pass.

It is certain, no matter how you approach the subject, that the counsel and advice he gave the king was the product of his deliberate operation of the gift of the word wisdom.

Via the operation of this gift, Daniel showed king Nebuchadnezzar what to do to avoid the sure judgement which was coming his way. (Incidentally, the judgement and the fact that it was coming had been revealed by the operation of the gift of the word of knowledge.)

Wherefore, O king, let my counsel be acceptable unto thee, and break off thy sins by righteousness, and thine iniquities by shewing mercy to the poor; if it may be a lengthening of thy tranquillity.

Daniel 4:27

As Moses led his people into the wilderness toward Canaan, his father-law, Jethro, high priest of Midian, came to visit.

And it came to pass on the morrow, that Moses sat to judge the people: and the people stood by Moses from the morning unto the evening.

And when Moses' father in law saw all that he did to the people, he said, What is this thing that thou doest to the people? Why sittest thou thyself alone, and all the people stand by thee from morning unto even?

And Moses said unto his father in law, Because the people come unto me to enquire of God:

When they have a matter, they come unto me; and I judge between one and another, and I do make them know the statutes of God, and his laws.

Exodus 18:13-16

At this time Jethro gave his son-in-law counsel and advice to the end that he and the nation might survive and make progress in their march toward the land God had promised them.

And Moses' father in law said unto him, The thing that thou doest is not good.

Thou wilt surely wear away, both thou, and this people that is with thee: for this thing is too heavy for thee; thou art not able to perform it thyself alone.
Hearken now unto my voice, I will give thee counsel, and God shall be with thee: Be thou for the people to God-ward, that thou mayest bring the causes unto God:

And thou shalt teach them ordinances and laws, and shalt shew them the way wherein they must walk, and the work that they must do.

Moreover thou shalt provide out of all the people able men, such as fear God, men of truth, hating covetousness; and place such over them, to be rulers of thousands, and rulers of hundreds, rulers of fifties, and rulers of tens:

And let them judge the people at all seasons: and it shall be, that every great matter they shall bring unto thee, but every small matter they shall judge: so shall it be easier for thyself, and they shall bear the burden with thee.

If thou shalt do this thing, and God command thee so, then thou shalt be able to endure, and all this people shall also go to their place in peace.

Exodus 18:17-23

Even a casual survey of the above Scriptures will suffice to convince any open heart that Jethro's counsel was the product of the operation of the gift of the word of wisdom.

Joshua had this gift.

And Joshua the son of Nun was full of the spirit of wisdom; for Moses had laid his hands upon him: and the children of Israel hearkened unto him, and did as the LORD commanded Moses.
Deuteronomy 34:9

This verse also states that he received this gift by the laying on of hands of Moses. It all happened when God spoke to Moses concerning his death and the appointing of a successor.

And the LORD said unto Moses, Take thee Joshua the son of Nun, a man in whom is the spirit, and lay thine hand upon him;

And set him before Eleazar the priest, and before all the congregation; and give him a charge in their sight.

And thou shalt put some of thine honour upon him, that all the congregation of the children of Israel may be obedient.

And he shall stand before Eleazar the priest, who shall ask counsel for him after the judgment of Urim before the LORD: at his word shall they go out, and at his word they shall come in, both he, and all the children of Israel with him, even all the congregation.

And Moses did as the LORD commanded him: and he took Joshua, and set him before Eleazar the priest, and before all the congregation:

And he laid his hands upon him, and gave him a charge, as the LORD commanded by the hand of Moses.
Numbers 27:18-23

Note: "The Spirit of wisdom" is Old Testament phraseology for the gift of the word of wisdom.

Solomon prayed for the gift of the word of wisdom and the gift of the word of knowledge.

> **In that night did God appear unto Solomon, and said unto him, Ask what I shall give thee.**
>
> **And Solomon said unto God, Thou hast shewed great mercy unto David my father, and hast made me to reign in his stead.**
>
> **Now, O LORD God, let thy promise unto David my father be established: for thou hast made me king over a people like the dust of the earth in multitude.**
> **Give me now wisdom and knowledge, that I may go out and come in before this people: for who can judge this thy people, that is so great?**
>
>

II Chronicles 1:7-10

God was pleased with the request of Solomon so much so that He not only granted it, He added to the young king much more.

> **And God said to Solomon, Because this was in thine heart, and thou hast not asked riches, wealth, or honour, nor the life of thine enemies, neither yet hast asked long life; but hast asked wisdom and knowledge for thyself, that thou mayest judge my people, over whom I have made thee king:**
>
> **Wisdom and knowledge is granted unto thee; and I will give thee riches, and wealth, and honour, such as none of the kings have had that have been before thee, neither shall there any after thee have the like.**
>
>

II Chronicles 1:11-12

CHAPTER FIVE
QUESTIONS

1. This gift works in conjunction with which gift?

_____

_____

2. The gift of the word of wisdom was used by many in the Bible. Give some Scripture references and explain in your own words their accomplishments:

Jesus

_____

_____

_____

_____

_____

Solomon

_____

_____

_____

_____

_____

James

_____

_____

_____

_____

_____

3. List some of the attributes of the gift of the word of wisdom.

_____

_____

_____

_____

4. This gift is full of:

_____

_____

5. List two elements that this gift is without:

_____

_____

CHAPTER SIX

THE GIFT OF THE DISCERNING OF SPIRITS

And they shall teach my people the difference between the holy and profane, and cause them to discern between the unclean and the clean.

Ezekiel 44:23

WHAT IT IS NOT:

It is not the gift of discerment; there is no such gift. Discernment is astuteness in judgment, insight, a purely natural ability. It is not the gift of criticism, neither is it the gift of suspicion.

WHAT IT IS:

It is the God-given ability to detect the presence and ascertain the identity of spirits, and spirits only. There is such a thing as the gift of discerning of men.

One should not confuse the discerning of spirits with the casting out of devils. The casting out of devils is an act on the part of the believer ministering. The gift of the discerning of spirits is the God-given ability to perform a certain act, but the act is the discerning, not the casting out of spirits.

Now to disuss this gift properly, an understanding (at lease in part) of spirits is required. The subject is a vast one.

ALL LIFE IS SPIRIT

There is a spirit in man...Job 32:8

In the beginning:

And the LORD God formed man of the dust of the ground, and breathed into his nostrils the breath of life; and man became a living soul.

Genesis 2:7

The breath of life is known as
the spirit of man which is in him....1Cor. 2:11

This life (all spirit is life and all life is spirit) is in the blood.

For the life of the flesh is in the blood.

Leviticus 17:11

It is this life (spirit) in a man which keeps him alive. By the same token, death is the departing of that spirit (life). This is attested to by the Word of God in connection with the raising of the daughter of Jairus from the dead.

And he put them all out, and took her by the hand, and called, saying, Maid, arise.

And her spirit came again, and she arose straightway: and he commanded to give her meat.

Luke 8:54-55

When a person dies, the spirit (life) leaves the body. Having come from God in the first place, it nows returns to Him.

Then shall the dust return to the earth as it was: and the spirit shall return unto God who gave it.

At death, the spirit of man goes up.

Who knoweth the spirit of man that goeth upward, and the spirit of the beast that goeth downward to the earth?
                                        Ecclesiastes 3:21

In the beginning man was made.

And God said, let us make man...Gen. 1:26

To make anything, substance is required.

And the LORD God formed man of the dust of the ground, and breathed into his nostrils the breath of life; and man became a living soul.
                                        Genesis 2:7

The Almighty took dust of the earth, formed it into a shape, and declared that shape was the "form" of man. Therefore that "form" was, and is, the "form" of man. This word is commonly used in the Scriptures to designate man's body, his design, etc. It is also used much in making plain the fact that man is actually God's handiwork.

Adam was first formed, then Eve. ...1Tim. 2:13

David, in one of his most outsiding psalms, declares that God

formed the eye...Psalms 94:9

Ehihu testifies to the same truth.

The Spirit of God hath made me...

Continuing his testimony, he declares:

the breath of the Almighty hath given me life. (Job 33:4)

He makes a further statement to the effect that God fashioned him, and fashioned him of earth.

I also am formed out of clay Job.33:6

In the book of the prophet Isaiah, God sums up the entire matter conclusively. Speaking of the bringing of man into existence He says:

Even every one that is called by my name: for I have created him for my glory, I have formed him; yea, I have made him.
Isaiah 43:7

That God made man, formed man, and created man, there can be no vestige of doubt. That these terms are not synonymous is just as apparent. To make, one requires substances. The thing made must, of necessity, be given some sort of shape; it must be formed. When one creates, he produces something out of nothing.

God, therefore did not create man's body. He made it; He formed it; of the dust of the earth He produced it. What He created was in His (God's) image. Man's body is not in the image of God. It is in the form of man.

Nevertherless man, says the Word, was created in the image of God.

So God created man in his own image, in the image of God created he him; male and female created he them.
Genesis 1:27

God is a Spirit.....John 4:24

Therefore, that part of man which He (God) created is spirit.

The fall of man from his original state demanded a new creation within his being before fellowship with God could be restored. This new creation is the new birth which one experiences through faith in the finished work of Christ., i.e., that which He accomplished for us by the substitutionary death upon the cross.

A Christian therefore, is a person in whom a new spirit exists, i.e., the spirit of Christ.

> **But ye are not in the flesh, but in the Spirit, if so be that the Spirit of God dwell in you. Now if any man have not the Spirit of Christ, he is none of his.**
> **Romans 8:9**

By the same token, if you are one of His, you have His spirit; this is that new spirit which has come into existence and being in your heart.

> **Therefore if any man be in Christ, he is a new creature: old things are passed away; behold, all things are become new.**
> **2 Corinthians 5:17**

This is that new man:

> **And that ye put on the new man, which after God is created in righteousness and true holiness.**
> **Ephesians 4:24**

This new man is created in the image of God:

> **And have put on the new man, which is renewed in knowledge after the image of him that created him:**
> **Colossians 3:10**

Angels are spirits. The Word of God makes this plain.

And of the angels he saith, Who maketh his angels spirits, and his ministers a flame of fire.

Hebrews 1:7

God created them all. But there was war in heaven. Lucifer, brightest of the sons of the morning, second only to God Almighty Himself in power, beauty, and wisdom, rebelled against his Creator, and cajoled one third of the heavenly host into rebellion also.

And there was war in heaven:

And there was war in heaven: Michael and his angels fought against the dragon; and the dragon fought and his angels,

And prevailed not; neither was their place found any more in heaven.

And the great dragon was cast out, that old serpent, called the Devil, and Satan, which deceiveth the whole world: he was cast out into the earth, and his angels were cast out with him.

Revelation 12:7-9

The reason for the rebellion was from Lucifer's desire to usurp God's throne, and to be as God Himself.

For thou hast said in thine heart, I will ascend into heaven, I will exalt my throne above the stars of God: I will sit also upon the mount of the congregation, in the sides of the north:

I will ascend above the heights of the clouds; I will be like the most High.

Isaiah 14:13-14

Satan was Lucifer falling from heaven.

How art thou fallen from heaven, O Lucifer, son of the morning! how art thou cut down to the ground, which didst weaken the nations!
Isaiah 14:12

He, Lucifer, is now known as the Devil, and Satan. The angels that fell with him are known as his, this automatically leaving him in complete control of them all. Hell was prepared specificallly for them.

... everlasting fire, prepared for the devil and his angels:
Matthew 25:41

The spirit world, therefore, spreads itself before us, a great panorama. There is God Himself, Who always was, and Who always will be. He is a spirit. He alone is holy. He is the Holy Spirit.

There are the angels of God: Michael the Archangel; Gabriel, who is known in the Scriptures as the angel of the Lord; and multitudes of other angels, millions of created spirits, all good.

There is the spirit of man in each man. There are those who are born; in each one of these dwells a new spirit, a spirit which is born of God, created in His image.

There are the millions of fallen angels, and Lucifer himself, now known as Satan and the Devil. Besides all this, the Lord God spoke to the serpent (Satan himself) in the garden of Eden and, while declaring judgement upon him for the part he played in procuring the fall of men, mentioned his seed.

And I will put enmity between thee and the woman, and between thy seed and her seed; it shall bruise thy head, and thou shalt bruise his heel.

Genesis 3:15

Four thousand years later, Christ faced a group of priests in the temple at Jerusalem.

I know that ye are Abraham's seed; but ye seek to kill me, because my word hath no place in you.

I speak that which I have seen with my Father: and ye do that which ye have seen with your father.

They answered and said unto him, Abraham is our father. Jesus saith unto them, If ye were Abraham's children, ye would do the works of Abraham.

But now ye seek to kill me, a man that hath told you the truth, which I have heard of God: this did not Abraham.

Ye do the deeds of your father. Then said they to him, We be not born of fornication; we have one Father, even God.

Jesus said unto them, If God were your Father, ye would love me: for I proceeded forth and came from God; neither came I of myself, but he sent me.

Why do ye not understand my speech? even because ye cannot hear my word.

Ye are of your father the devil, and the lusts of your father ye will do. He was a murderer from the beginning, and abode not in the

truth, because there is no truth in him. When he speaketh a lie, he speaketh of his own: for he is a liar, and the father of it.
John 8:37-44

Jesus acknowledged them as Abraham's seed, yet declared Abraham was not their father, and finally declared them to be their father the devil.

Jesus was not using a figure of speech here. Rather, He was being very specific. He was not adddressing the flesh when He called them the seed of the serpent, but was addressing the evil spirits resident in these men. These evil spirits were not fallen angels, for such cannot be the seed of Satan: they were created by God Almighty. These spirits were begotten of Satan. They were his offspring, his seed.

So our spirit world has grown. And the two great camps therein are opposed the one to the other as diametrically as day and night are opposed the one to the other.

In the spirit world, therefore, a great and continuous battle rages. It is between God Almighty with His angels of heaven and Satan with his hosts. Man (natural man) understands it not.

But the natural man receiveth not the things of the Spirit of God: for they are foolishness unto him: neither can he know them, because they are spiritually discerned.
1 Corinthians 2:14

God has not left His people helpless against the onslaughts of the enemy. He has provided spiritual armament and armour for us whom He has called into this battle with Him, and He exhorts us to put it on.

Finally, my brethren, be strong in the Lord, and in the power of his might.

Put on the whole armour of God, that ye may be able to stand against the wiles of the devil.

For we wrestle not against flesh and blood, but against principalities, against powers, against the rulers of the darkness of this world, against spiritual wickedness in high places.

Wherefore take unto you the whole armour of God, that ye may be able to withstand in the evil day, and having done all, to stand.

Stand therefore, having your loins girt about with truth, and having on the breastplate of righteousness;

And your feet shod with the preparation of the gospel of peace;

Above all, taking the shield of faith, wherewith ye shall be able to quench all the fiery darts of the wicked.

And take the helmet of salvation, and the sword of the Spirit, which is the word of God:

Ephesians 6:10-17

God fully understands our inability to cope with supernatural forces in our natural strength and wisdom. Therefore, He has provided supernatural abilities, the gifts of the Spirit, and He says to us concerning them:

Now concerning spiritual gifts, brethren, I would not have you ignorant.

1 Corinthians 12:1

He says unto us:

Behold, I give unto you power to tread on serpents and scorpions, and over all the power of the enemy: and nothing shall by any means hurt you.
Luke 10:19

His Word declares that we shall receive power after we have been baptized with the Holy Ghost.

But ye shall receive power, after that the Holy Ghost is come upon you: and ye shall be witnesses unto me both in Jerusalem, and in all Judaea, and in Samaria, and unto the uttermost part of the earth.
Acts 1:8

Far too many of God's people do not realize that the term "power" as it is used here, signifies ability. It could as well be written: I make you able. It means the same thing; able to cast out devils; able to heal the sick; able ministers of the new covenant. This infers the receiving and utilization of spiritual gifts, i.e., God-given abilities, for by these and your use of them only are you made able; only by your deliberate use of them have you power over the enemy.

God intended us to receive and utilize the gifts of the spirit to the tearing down of the strongholds of Satan.

For though we walk in the flesh, we do not war after the flesh:

(For the weapons of our warfare are not carnal, but mighty through God to the pulling down of strong holds;)

Casting down imaginations, and every high thing that exalteth itself against the knowledge of God, and bringing into captivity every thought to the obedience of Christ;

2 Corinthians 10:3-5

The weapons of our warfare are the gifts of the spirit. These, and all truths connected therewith, are revealed unto us by the Spirit of God.

But as it is written, Eye hath not seen, nor ear heard, neither have entered into the heart of man, the things which God hath prepared for them that love him.

But God hath revealed them unto us by his Spirit: for the Spirit searcheth all things, yea, the deep things of God.

1 Corinthians 2:9-10

Now we have received, not the spirit of the world, but the spirit which is of God; that we might know the things that are freely given to us of God.

Which things also we speak, not in the words which man's wisdom teacheth, but which the Holy Ghost teacheth; comparing spiritual things with spiritual.

1 Corinthians 2:12-13

While it is true that the things of the Spirit (and of the spirit world) are not read to the mind of man - natural man - they are nevertheless real, and discernible. However, God's Word makes it plain that this is only accomplished by spiritual means. The efforts of our natural man are futile.

But the natural man receiveth not the things of the Spirit of God: for they are foolishness unto him: neither can he know them, because they are spiritually discerned.

1 Corinthians 2:14

The same principle applies to the understanding of the spirit world.

Our securtity lie in seeing nothing, recognizing nothing, after the flesh (the natural man); in knowing nothing (spiritually speaking) thereby.

Wherefore henceforth know we no man after the flesh: yea, though we have known Christ after the flesh, yet now henceforth know we him no more.
2 Corinthians 5:16

This is accomplished by the use of the gift of the discerning of spirits: the God-given ability to detect the presence and acertain the identity of spirits, whether they be good or bad.

The gift of the discerning of spirits is not by any means the least of the spiritual abilities. It is the God-given ability to detect the presence and acertain the identity of spirits, whether God who is the Holy Spirit; the spirit of man which is in man; the Spirit of Christ, that new creature in you; one or more of the angels of glory; one or more of the spirits of hell or Satan himself.

We see this gift in operation in John the Baptist, referring to certain people as a generation of vipers: snakes, not sheep.

Then said he to the multitude that came forth to be baptized of him, O generation of vipers, who hath warned you to flee from the wrath to come?
Luke 3:7

John was certainly not addressing their flesh, any more than Jesus was when He declared that those priests in the temple were seed of the serpent.

Jesus called certain Pharisees vipers.

O generation of vipers....Matt. 12:34

On another occasion He did likewise, this time including the appellation "serpents".

Ye serpents, ye generation of vipers...Matt.23:33

When freeing the woman from a spirit of infirmity, (which He discerned,) He was able to declare that Satan himself had bound her with it.

And, behold, there was a woman which had a spirit of infirmity eighteen years, and was bowed together, and could in no wise lift up herself.

And when Jesus saw her, he called her to him, and said unto her, Woman, thou art loosed from thine infirmity.

And he laid his hands on her: and immediately she was made straight, and glorified God.
                                                Luke 13:11-13

CHAPTER SIX
QUESTIONS

1. How does casting out demons make use of the gift of the discerning of spirit?

_____
_____
_____
_____
_____

2. Give examples when this gift was used by:

     Jesus

_____
_____
_____
_____

     Paul

_____
_____
_____
_____

     Peter

_____
_____
_____
_____

3. How close is this God-given gift to that of the evil spirit world practices?

_____

_____

_____

_____

_____

_____

_____

4. Where do evil spirits abide in man?

_____

_____

_____

_____

_____

_____

_____

5. Some cases of epilepsy are caused by evil spirits. Find a case in the Bible in which it was.

_____

_____

_____

_____

_____

_____

_____

_____

6. Differentiate the spirit man, the spirit of God and evil spirits.

_____

_____

_____

_____

_____

_____

_____

7. What Scripture indicates Paul addressing Timothy about this gift?

_____

_____

_____

_____

_____

_____

_____

8. When, in the local church, can this gift be actively used?

_____

_____

_____

_____

_____

_____

_____

_____

_____

PART THREE

THE POWER GIFTS OF THE SPIRIT

PRELIMINARY

The third and last group of the supernatural abilities (i.e., the power gifts of the Spirit) are so called because they operate by the power of God. This is the power in and by which Paul preached the gospel to the heathen and wrought the signs which confirmed it to their hearts.

For I will not dare to speak of any of those things which Christ hath not wrought by me, to make the Gentiles obedient, by word and deed,

Through mighty signs and wonders, by the power of the Spirit of God; so that from Jerusalem, and round about unto Illyricum, I have fully preached the gospel of Christ.
Romans 15:18-19

Paul declares that it was according to the effectual working of God's power that he was made a minister of the gospel of God's grace.

Whereof I was made a minister, according to the gift of the grace of God given unto me by the effectual working of his power.
Ephesians 3:7

He likewise declares that while God is able to do exceeding abundantly on our behalf, yet it is according to His power working in us.

Now unto him that is able to do exceeding abundantly above all that we ask or think, according to the power that worketh in us,
Ephesians 3:20

Paul states further that the work of the ministry will only be accomplished by that which every child of God contributes in the supernatural realm. He makes it very plain that this is supplied according to the effectiveness of the working of the power of God in us.

From whom the whole body fitly joined together and compacted by that which every joint supplieth, according to the effectual working in the measure of every part, maketh increase of the body unto the edifying of itself in love.
Ephesians 4:16

We can readily see here the need for the gifts of the Spirit. However, we see also that without the power of God in us, and our effectual use of it, we will never accomplish that which God has planned for us to accomplish. Jesus promised that we should have that power after we were baptized with the Holy Ghost.

But ye shall receive power, after that the Holy Ghost is come upon you: and ye shall be witnesses unto me both in Jerusalem, and in all Judaea, and in Samaria, and unto the uttermost part of the earth.
Acts 1:8

Once we have received this power, it is in us.

But we have this treasure in earthen vessels, that the excellency of the power may be of God, and not of us.
2 Corinthians 4:7

This power (this tresure) is necessary for the effective operation of the third group of the supernatural abilities. For this reason they are commonly referred to as the **power gifts of the Spirit.**

This group of spiritual gifts are also called **impartation gifts**. This is because by your deliberate operation of them you impart something to others, or, (putting it another way), something goes out from you to others.

When the woman with the issue of blood touched Jesus and was instantly healed, He said:

...I perceive that virtue is gone out of me. Luke 8:46B

Another time, Jesus was ministering in a great plain, and multitudes came to hear Him, and to be healed of their infirmities.

And the whole multitude sought to touch him: for there went virtue out of him, and healed them all.
Luke 6:19

When Peter and John stood facing the need of the cripple who spent his time begging at the Beautiful Gate of the Temple in Jerusalem, Peter said;

... such as I have give I thee.   Acts 3:6B

Here we have a concrete case of a man of God imparting something, something he possessed, to another. That this was something which met the need of the recipient (Who never had walked) enabling him to leap to his feet and walk, is made evident by the content.

And he took him by the right hand, and lifted him up: and immediately his feet and ankle bones received strength.

And he leaping up stood, and walked, and entered with them into the temple, walking, and leaping, and praising God.
Acts 3:7-8

Incidentally, Peter is the sacred writer who wrote:

If any man speak, let him speak as the oracles of God; if any man minister, let him do it as of the ability which God giveth: that

God in all things may be glorified through Jesus Christ, to whom be praise and dominion for ever and ever. Amen.
1 Peter 4:11

The ability given to us of God are the gifts of the Spirit, and it is evident that in this quotation Peter is referring to the **power or impartation gifts of the Spirit.**

These power or impartation gifts of the Spirit are three in number. We list them here in their proper sequence or order.

POWER OR IMPARTATION GIFTS:

1. The gift of **Faith.**
2. The gift of **Healing**.
3. The gift of the performing of **Miracles.**

We shall study them in this, their proper order.

CHAPTER SEVEN

THE GIFT OF FAITH

But without faith it is impossible to please him: for he that cometh to God must believe that he is, and that he is a rewarder of them that diligently seek him.
Hebrews 11:6

WHAT IT IS NOT

The gift of faith is not a different faith, another kind of faith. To say so is to manifest the grossest type of ignorance. Faith is faith; faith is substance; faith is evidence.

Now faith is the substance of things hoped for, the evidence of things not seen.
Hebrews 11:1

Faith is belief, which when acted upon to receive from God, becomes the evidence of that which you have not received as yet. Yes, faith is the substance and likewise the evidence; but we are not studying these. We are studying an ability; a supernatural ability; the ability to do certain specific things with that substance, thereby producing the evidence.

WHAT IT IS

The gift of faith, one of the nine gifts of the spirit, is the God-given ability to believe for the fantastically impossible to come to pass (and that at your word,) and the further ability to impart faith to others.

BELIEVE FOR THE IMPOSSIBLE TO COME TO PASS

We see this gift in this phase of its operations in the ministry of Jesus Himself when He cursed the fig tree.

And on the morrow, when they were come from Bethany, he was hungry:

And seeing a fig tree afar off having leaves, he came, if haply he might find any thing thereon: and when he came to it, he found nothing but leaves; for the time of figs was not yet.

And Jesus answered and said unto it, No man eat fruit of thee hereafter for ever. And his disciples heard it.
Mark 11:12-14

The next morning Peter noticed that the tree was dead, dried up from the roots. He drew Christ's attention to this phenomenon.

And Jesus answering saith unto them, Have faith in God.

For verily I say unto you, That whosoever shall say unto this mountain, Be thou removed, and be thou cast into the sea; and shall not doubt in his heart, but shall believe that those things which he saith shall come to pass; he shall have whatsoever he saith.
Mark 11:22-23

Now let us take a closer look at the latter part of that answer, reviewing it statement by statement:

1.   *Whosever shall say unto this mountain,* Christ taught, in this phrase, that we should address ourselves to the problem, to the need rather than to God with reference to the need.

2.   *Be thou removed.* Here we have the command. It goes without saying, that what Christ was placing before us here was authority, our authority in Him. We are authorized to command. The implied thought is, of course, that our commands shall be obeyed.

3.   *And shall not doubt in his heart.* There is no place for doubt in the economy of God. To doubt is to create rebellion within the heart of that one unto whom the command is addressed. Whatever we accomplish in Christ Jesus, is accomplished by faith. We accomplish nothing otherwise or by any other means. Doubt is the opposite of faith. To doubt, therefore, would be to war against one's own effort. Thus the one issuing the command would defeat his own purpose.

4.   *But shall believe that those things which he saith shall come to pass;* To successfully command demands with the heart of the one issuing the command implicit faith that the word spoken shall be obeyed. That which we are within, is manifest by that which proceeds from our lips. This embraces more, much more than the phrases employed. The manner in which our command is issued, the tone of voice, inflection, accompanying gestures etc., all speak loudly our implicit faith in the fact that we expect our command to be fulfilled, or betray our doubt that it will be.

5.   *He shall have whatever he saith.* The man who produces the result, is that man who, banishing all doubt from his inward parts, believes that without equivocation, every command he issues shall be obeyed, and to the letter.

That Christ is referring to the exercise of the gift of faith is made evident by the following from the pen of Paul.

... though I have all faith, so that I could remove mountains,
I Corinthians 13:2C

The context proves that Paul was speaking about the gift of faith. The mountain-moving infers this.

On one occasion, Christ's chosen ones, the twelve, asked Him for a larger portion of faith. His reply was a confirmation of all the foregoing. And the Apostles said unto the Lord, "increase our faith".

And the apostles said unto the Lord, Increase our faith.

And the Lord said, If ye had faith as a grain of mustard seed, ye might say unto this sycamine tree, Be thou plucked up by the root, and be thou planted in the sea; and it should obey you.
Luke 17:5-6

And Jesus, in another place, said unto them:

And Jesus said unto them, Because of your unbelief: for verily I say unto you, If ye have faith as a grain of mustard seed, ye shall say unto this mountain, Remove hence to yonder place; and it shall remove; and nothing shall be impossible unto you.
Matthew 17:20

Jesus not only utilized the gift of faith in its first or primal phase when He cursed the fig tree; He taught His disciples how to do likewise. There is no doubt that they learned their lesson well there is no doubt. Even a casual study of their lives and ministries will make that evident.

The Word of God implies that Barnabas possessed this gift of faith.

Then tidings of these things came unto the ears of the church which was in Jerusalem: and they sent forth Barnabas, that he should go as far as Antioch.

Who, when he came, and had seen the grace of God, was glad, and exhorted them all, that with purpose of heart they would cleave unto the Lord.

For he was a good man, and full of the Holy Ghost and of faith: and much people was added unto the Lord.
Acts 11:22-24

In Paul's second letter to Timothy he exhorts him to stir up a gift of the Spirit which he says is in him by the laying on of his hands.

Wherefore I put thee in remembrance that thou stir up the gift of God, which is in thee by the putting on of my hands.
II Timothy 1:6

A study of the context proves that this could be nothing less than the gift of faith.

When I call to remembrance the unfeigned faith that is in thee, which dwelt first in thy grandmother Lois, and thy mother Eunice; and I am persuaded that in thee also.
II Timothy 1:5

When Peter and John healed the crippled at the temple gate in the city of Jerusalem, the use of the gift of faith in this phase of its operations is very evident.

In the name of Jesus Christ of Nazareth rise up and walk.
Acts 3:6c

No praying, no begging, no supplicating, here! Peter commands in the name of the Lord, and the work is done. Note the similarity between his handling of this case and Christ's commanding of the fig tree.

CHAPTER SEVEN
QUESTIONS

1. Jesus often taught of using the gift of faith. Find some Scriptures that support this.

_____

_____

_____

_____

_____

_____

_____

2. Find some Scriptures that demonstrate this God-given ability in:

    - the Roman centurian

_____

_____

_____

_____

    - Jairus

_____

_____

_____

_____

    - the man at the gate Beautiful

_____

_____

_____

_____

3. How is one's belief tied into the gift of faith? Give illustrations for your answer.

_____
_____
_____
_____

4. How does the gift of faith relate to:

    a.) one that God is using to perform miracles

_____
_____
_____
_____

    b.) one receiving a miracle

_____
_____
_____
_____

5. How has this gift influenced your walk with God? Give examples how this gift caused you to be victorious.

_____
_____
_____
_____
_____
_____
_____

CHAPTER EIGHT

THE GIFT OF HEALING

.... they shall lay hands on the sick, and they shall recover.
Mark 16:18c

WHAT IT IS NOT

It is not a Midas touch. That is, there is no such thing as a gift that makes possible for one to heal others automatically, as though one were a healing machine. Faith is always to be reckoned with.

... without faith it is impossible to please him (God).
Hebrews 11:6

It is not a sensation, nor a sign, in the hand or in any other part of the body.

It is not a ministry of healing. We are studying a gift, not a ministry.

It is not a gift of healing. The Scripture makes reference to gifts of healing (I Corinthians 12:9B).

Many are confused concerning this, but only because of misinterpretation. Some claim this infers that one has a gift to heal burns, another a gift for the measles, etc. No wonder physicians laugh! The truth of the matter is that every healing is a gift — every healing you or anyone else has ever received or ever will receive. But we are not studying "a" gift of healing. You may have received many of them. We are studying "the" gift of healing. This quite a different subject.

WHAT IT IS

The gift of healing is the God-given ability to impart the healing virtue of Jesus Christ to others. Healing is a vast subject in itself, without taking thought concerning the ability to impart healing virtue.

The priests and prophets of Old Testament days ministered healing. Eli ministered to Hannah regarding her barrenness, and she was an outstanding case of deliverance and healing.

And she was in bitterness of soul, and prayed unto the LORD, and wept sore.

And she vowed a vow, and said, O LORD of hosts, if thou wilt indeed look on the affliction of thine handmaid, and remember me, and not forget thine handmaid, but wilt give unto thine handmaid a man child, then I will give him unto the LORD all the days of his life, and there shall no razor come upon his head.

And it came to pass, as she continued praying before the LORD, that Eli marked her mouth.

Now Hannah, she spake in her heart; only her lips moved, but her voice was not heard: therefore Eli thought she had been drunken.

And Eli said unto her, How long wilt thou be drunken? Put away thy wine from thee.

And Hannah answered and said, No, my lord, I am a woman of a sorrowful spirit: I have drunk neither wine nor strong drink, but have poured out my soul before the LORD.

Count not thine handmaid for a daughter of Belial: for out of the abundance of my complaint and grief have I spoken hitherto.

Then Eli answered and said, Go in peace: and the God of Israel grant thee thy petition that thou hast asked of him.
I Samuel 1:10-17

That her petition was answered according to his word is ample manifested.

And they rose up in the morning early, and worshipped before the LORD, and returned, and came to their house to Ramah: and Elkanah knew Hannah his wife; and the LORD remembered her.

Wherefore it came to pass, when the time was come about after Hannah had conceived, that she bare a son, and called his name Samuel, saying, Because I have asked him of the LORD.
I Samuel 1:19-20

David was a miracle of healing, and he bore testimony to the fact.

I will extol thee, O LORD; for thou hast lifted me up, and hast not made my foes to rejoice over me.

O LORD my God, I cried unto thee, and thou hast healed me.

O LORD, thou hast brought up my soul from the grave: thou hast kept me alive, that I should not go down to the pit.
Psalm 30:1-3

Hezekiah was a miracle of deliverance and healing, after inspired utterance had declared that he would die!

In those days was Hezekiah sick unto death. And Isaiah the prophet the son of Amoz came unto him, and said unto him, Thus saith the LORD, Set thine house in order: for thou shalt die, and not live.

Then Hezekiah turned his face toward the wall, and prayed unto the LORD,

And said, Remember now, O LORD, I beseech thee, how I have walked before thee in truth and with a perfect heart, and have done that which is good in thy sight. And Hezekiah wept sore.

Then came the word of the LORD to Isaiah, saying,

Go, and say to Hezekiah, Thus saith the LORD, the God of David thy father, I have heard thy prayer, I have seen thy tears: behold, I will add unto thy days fifteen years.
Isaiah 38:1-5

There are many more cases of healing recorded in the Old Testament, but these few will answer our purpose well. They have been chosen because they differ so. In every case the mode employed was different; but the results were the same.

CHAPTER EIGHT
QUESTIONS

1. Jesus Christ displayed abundantly the gift of healing in His ministry. Give examples and Scripture references to back this up.

_____

_____

_____

_____

_____

_____

_____

2. Find where this gift was exercised by:

    a.) the apostles

_____

_____

_____

_____

_____

    b.) Philip

_____

_____

_____

_____

_____

    c.) Peter

_____

_____

_____

_____

    d.) Paul

_____

_____

_____

_____

3. When was Paul a recepient of the use of this gift?

_____

_____

4. Match the following:

    a. to restore to health   _____ a bringing together

    b. to cure   _____ to make completely whole

    c. to make sound   _____ one has once known health and been robbed of it

    d. to reconcile   _____ to set free from or remove the cause of a condition

CHAPTER NINE

THE GIFT OF THE PERFORMING OF MIRACLES

Verily, verily, I say unto you, He that believeth on me, the works that I do shall he do also; and greater works than these shall he do; because I go unto my Father.

John 14:12

WHAT IT IS NOT

It is not the gift of miracles. There is no such gift. It is the gift of the performing of miracles. Let us be careful about the phraseology we employ when we refer to any of the gifts of the Spirit. Faulty phraseology here may beget false doctrine later. It is the father of much of the confusion existent today among God's people concerning spiritual gifts.

WHAT IT IS

Before we can properly declare what the gift of the performing of miracles actually is, we shall have to know what constitutes a miracle. A miracle is a supernatural act or occurrence: that which is contrary to or beyond realm of the laws of nature. The gift of the performing of miracles, therefore, is the God-given ability to perform, to cause to come to pass, acts that are supernatural, that are beyond the realm of or contrary to the laws of nature.

We see this gift in operation in the ministry of Moses as he turns his rod into a serpent and vice versa.

And Moses answered and said, But, behold, they will not believe me, nor hearken unto my voice: for they will say, The LORD hath not appeared unto thee.

And the LORD said unto him, What is that in thine hand? And he said, A rod.

And he said, Cast it on the ground. And he cast it on the ground, and it became a serpent; and Moses fled from before it.

And the LORD said unto Moses, Put forth thine hand, and take it by the tail. And he put forth his hand, and caught it, and it became a rod in his hand:

Exodus 4:1-4

And Moses and Aaron did so, as the LORD commanded; and he lifted up the rod, and smote the waters that were in the river, in the sight of Pharaoh, and in the sight of his servants; and all the waters that were in the river were turned to blood.

Exodus 7:20

And the LORD spake unto Moses, Say unto Aaron, Stretch forth thine hand with thy rod over the streams, over the rivers, and over the ponds, and cause frogs to come up upon the land of Egypt.

And Aaron stretched out his hand over the waters of Egypt; and the frogs came up, and covered the land of Egypt.

Exodus 8:5-6

Regarding the fact that the Lord told Moses to tell Aaron to stretch forth the rod over the water, there need be no confusion. Aaron simply stretched forth the rod (went through the motions); Moses produced the miracle. The Word of God is explicit concerning this fact. Nowhere in the Scriptures is Aaron referred to as having performed any miracles. Neither is there any record of his having been commissioned to perform any. On the other hand, Moses' commission is clear and distinct, and his miracle-working ministry is well attested to. Moreover, God commissioned Moses as a god unto Pharaoh. He then gave Aaron unto Moses as his (Moses') prophet.

And the LORD said unto Moses, See, I have made thee a god to Pharaoh: and Aaron thy brother shall be thy prophet.

Thou shalt speak all that I command thee: and Aaron thy brother shall speak unto Pharaoh, that he send the children of Israel out of his land.

Exodus 7:1-2

From this moment, until the deliverance of the Hebrews was an accomplished feat. Moses assumed the role and dignity of a supreme being whenever he was before Pharaoh. He ordered his prophet, Aaron, to do the works. Aaron complied. But we must return to Moses and his commission.

And the LORD said furthermore unto him, Put now thine hand into thy bosom. And he put his hand into his bosom: and when he took it out, behold, his hand was leprous as snow.

And he said, Put thine hand into thy bosom again. And he put his hand into his bosom again; and plucked it out of his bosom, and, behold, it was turned again as his other flesh.

And it shall come to pass, if they will not believe thee, neither hearken to the voice of the first sign, that they will believe the voice of the latter sign.

And it shall come to pass, if they will not believe also these two signs, neither hearken unto thy voice, that thou shalt take of the water of the river, and pour it upon the dry land: and the water which thou takest out of the river shall become blood upon the dry land.

Exodus 4:6-9

And the LORD said unto Moses, When thou goest to return into Egypt, see that thou do all those wonders before Pharaoh, which I have put in thine hand: but I will harden his heart, that he shall not let the people go.

Exodus 4:21

Moses wrought many more mighty miracles while he was in Egypt. Later, as they journeyed through the wilderness, he did other miracles, signs, and wonders. He sweetened the waters of Marah.

And when they came to Marah, they could not drink of the waters of Marah, for they were bitter: therefore the name of it was called Marah.

And the people murmured against Moses, saying, What shall we drink?

And he cried unto the LORD; and the LORD shewed him a tree, which when he had cast into the waters, the waters were made sweet: there he made for them a statute and an ordinance, and there he proved them,

Exodus 15:23-25

He brought forth water from the rock Horeb.

And the LORD said unto Moses, Go on before the people, and take with thee of the elders of Israel; and thy rod, wherewith thou smotest the river, take in thine hand, and go.

Behold, I will stand before thee there upon the rock in Horeb; and thou shalt smite the rock, and there shall come water out of it, that the people may drink. And Moses did so in the sight of the elders of Israel.

Exodus 17:5-6

You will have noticed that since leaving Egypt, Moses himself had literally produced the signs. No longer was he assuming the role of deity. No longer was Aaron his Prophet. For God was the God of the people, and Moses was His prophet. Obedient therefore to the word of his God, Moses produced the signs and the wonders.

After his death, his marvelous ministry received the honor of which it was worthy.

And there arose not a prophet since in Israel like unto Moses, whom the LORD knew face to face,

In all the signs and the wonders, which the LORD sent him to do in the land of Egypt to Pharaoh, and to all his servants, and to all his land,

And in all that mighty hand, and in all the great terror which Moses shewed in the sight of all Israel.
Deuteronomy 34:10-12

Before we continue, I would like to draw your attention to the fact that we are not studying miracles. We are studying the gift of the performing of miracles. Our subject matter, therefore, is chosen because it manifests the use of the gift of the performing of miracles.

CHAPTER NINE
QUESTIONS

1. List some of the manifestations of the gift of the performing of miracles in the life of:

    - Moses

_____

_____

_____

_____

    - Joshua

_____

_____

_____

_____

    - Elijah

_____

_____

_____

_____

    - Elisha

_____

_____

_____

- Jesus

_____
_____
_____
_____

- Paul

_____
_____
_____
_____

- the apostles

_____
_____
_____
_____

- God

_____
_____
_____
_____
_____

2. What is the difference between miracles and the gift of the performing of miracles?

_____
_____
_____
_____
_____
_____

3. Do we still see this gift in operation today? What have you personally witnessed in your life time, that used this gift?

_____

_____

_____

_____

_____

_____

_____

_____

_____

_____

_____

_____

_____

_____

_____

_____

_____

_____

_____

_____

_____

_____

_____

_____

_____

_____

To contact Dr. Charles Dixon for speaking
engagements, to conduct seminars or crusades,
please contact him at the following:

Dr. Charles Dixon
Charles Dixon Global Ministries
P.O. Box 34533
San Antonio, TX 78265

(210) 491-0255
(210) 491-0694 fax